THE AUSTRALIAN HISTORICAL RECIPE BOOK

by

John Caire

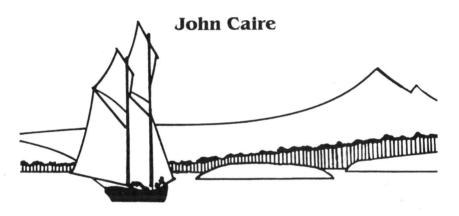

First published 1993 by Southern Holdings Pty Ltd
P.O. Box 6, Huonville 7109, Australia.
© **Copyright 1992 by Southern Holdings Pty Ltd**

ISBN 094 9089 24 9

This book is available from the publishers, Southern Holdings Pty Ltd,
P.O. Huonville 7109, for $5.95 plus $1.60 P.& P.
or Phone/Fax (002) 664112

Photographs supplied by: Apple & Heritage Museum, Grove;
Beattie's Studio; Maritime Museum, Hobart; Mrs. H.E. Bender; D. Hammond.

JOHN CAIRE has served as Chef and Manager in many famous Australian Hotels. After a prominent career in management, he returned to his first love, cooking, but this time as a restauranteur.

Everything he had a hand in became successful, award-winning, and very popular. At Franklin, a famous historic town, John's *Franklin Grill* is an exciting demonstration of the popularity of his cooking.

Contents

Page

3   **LIVING OFF THE LAND**
7   To Roast a Swan
     Kangaroo Stew
8   Baked Fish
9   Native Hen
     Wild Duck
     Scallops
10   Whitebait Fritters
     Boiled Crayfish Salad
     Abalone
     Potted Possum
11   Roast Lamb Head & Pluck
     Stewed Beef Kidney
     Brawn
12   Tripe in White Onion Sauce
     Dormers
     True Irish Stew
     Fried Ox Feet or Cow Heel
13   Stewed Oxtail
     Steak & Kidney Pudding
14   To Roast a Rabbit
15   Moulded Fowl
     Dresden Patties
     Fish Baked in Vinegar
16   Yorkshire Pudding
     Blackjack
     Boiled Tongue
     Baked Fish
     Kedgeree of Fish
17   Sassafras Beer
18   Fish Roe on Toast
     VEGETABLES
     Beetroot
     Cauliflower
     Cabbage
19   Broad Beans
     Celery
     French Beans
     Boiled Potatoes
     Lentils
     Spinach
     Vegetable Marrow
20   Carrots, Turnips & Swedes

Page

     JAMS, JELLIES & PICKLES
20   Candied Lemon Peel
     Marmalade
     Quince Jelly
21   Grape Jelly
     Pickled Onions
     Tomato Sauce
     Apple Chutney
22   Clear Green Tomato Pickle
     Pickled Red Cabbage or Cauli
     Pickled Walnuts
     SMOKING, SALT CURING & CANNING
     To Cure a Ham
23   Pickle for Beef
     Good Household Soap
     Pickled Eggs
24   **SHOVEL & STEAMBOAT COOKING**
     Shovel Fritters
     Bush Rissoles
     Continual Stew Stock Pot
25   **BREAD MAKING**
     Yeast
     Bread
26   Flour
     Millers' Bread
     Yeast Fruit Loaf
27   **DESSERTS, CONFECTIONERY & CAKES**
     Afternoon Tea Cakes
     Apple Cake
29   Afternoon Tea Scones
     Drop Scones
     Aunty's Patty Cakes
     Shortbread
30   Gingerbread
     Treacle Sponge
     Iced Cinnamon Cake
31   Sponge Cake
     Albert Pudding
     Jam or Golden Syrup Pudding

Contents

Page

32 Apple Charlotte
Gooseberry Fool
Cream Puffs
Trifle
33 Blancmange
Raspberry Cream
34 **CHRISTMAS SPECIALITIES**
Christmas Mince for Mince Pies
Christmas Pudding
Christmas Cake
35 **SWEETS & LOLLIES**
French Jellies
Baker's Toast
Coconut Ice
Marshmallows
Chocolate Almonds
36 Caramel Toffee
Marshmallow Cones
Russian Caramels
Peanut Brittle
Chocolate Toffee
37 Rice Bubbles & Date Fingers
Turkish Delight
THE FIFTIES & SIXTIES
38 Tuna Macaroni
Beef A La Mode
Lobster Thermidor
39 Spaghetti Bolognaise
Chicken Maryland
40 Glazed Hawaiian Ham Steaks
Hungarian Goulash
Tournados Rossini
41 Wiener Schnitzel
Creme Caramel
Zabaglione
42 Strawberries Romanoff
Rice Cream
Brandy Crusta
43 Lemon Meringue Pie
THE SEVENTIES & EIGHTIES
44 Satay
45 Saffron Rice
Fried Rice (Nasi Goreng)
Japanese Marinade Beef Teriyaki

Page

46 Vietnamese Clay Pot Squid
Seafood Steamboat
47 Indian Tandoori Chicken
Sushi
48 Gazpacho Soup
Quiche Lorraine
49 Cheese Souffle
Smoked Salmon Mousse
Waldorf Astoria Salad
50 **THE NINETIES & BEYOND**
Risotto of Asparagus, Scallops
& Lemon Balm
51 Pears Norzola - Stilton
Fish Fillets Steamed in Paperbark
for One
Wattle Mousse
Wattle Tea
52 Native Currant Dressing
Lillipilli Vinegar
Rosella Relish
Warrigal Greens and Potato Soup
Wichetty Grub Soup
53 Grilled Loin of Lamb
54 Atlantic Salmon & Chervil
Smoked Salmon & Caviar Pizza
55 Grilled Shitake Mushroom Salad
Olive Oil Mayonnaise
56 Vegetarian Salad with Grilled
Eggplant & Green Zucchini
Aioli
Pesto
57 Game Consomme with Poached
Quail Egg
Lemon Iced Souffle with
Raspberry Coulis
58 Onion Comfits with Barramundi
or Trevalla Fillets
Mancha Manteles (Pork with
Bananas & Peaches
Veal in Balsamic Vinegar
59 Measures
60 Cup & Spoon equivalents

Living Off The Land

Most Australian towns remember and revere their pioneers. In the Huon, where this book originated, this is especially so, for it was first settled in the 1830's, and because of its isolation until recent years many old buildings and artefacts still exist; the history is so recent that the descendants of some first settlement families still live on the original land grants. Of more practical importance is the existence of the recipe books the pioneers brought with them. From these, and from later family recipes over the years, and those used today by the author, a professional chef and restauranteur, this unique book of practical recipes is compiled.

Daily life for these settlers was one of hard toil and small rewards. One, Osborne Geeves, wrote:

"We lived in bark or slab huts we built for ourselves, and split shingles and laths at night to buy rations ... we worked the land in the day time, planted potatoes and grew vegetables of all kinds and lived on them largely. Raised a few fowls, your old mother making half a pound of butter a week from goat's milk ... dug eels out of swamps. In a year or two a cow was bought and some piglets reared on thistles till the potatoes, peas and beans grew. I have known a thrifty wife gather scotch thistles and boil them for the pigs. Fortunately there were no stores to give us credit; that saved us from luxurious ruin!"

Living in an environment where every commodity was precious, pioneer women learned to be excellent economists. This included such measures as keeping the scum from the top of corned beef for salting vegetables. Cooking was carried out over open fires with pots and kettles suspended on chains. They were hooked higher or lower on the chain to determine the rate of cooking. Baking was done in a camp oven - an iron vessel with a lid - which stood in the coals. Candles and soap were home made, and care had to be taken when rendering fat for the soap, that no salt remained, or the soap would not lather.

Water for washing clothes and for bathing had to be carried and heated over a fire. Ironing was done with solid flat irons heated in turn at the edge of the open fire. When it is considered how many clothes were worn, with petticoats, pinafores and cotton underwear with frills, the weekly washing and ironing was no light task.

In "The Romance of Dorset Hill," Edward Wallis wrote about his ancestors who settled "on the southern tip of Mount Misery above the fog level of the Huon Valley and on the fringe of the snow line." Their home was built of split timber and stone found on the site. The timber was shaped

The hay harvested and stacked - a 1906 picture.

An early 'Town House' - a cottage built 150 years ago from local hardwood.

4

by the axe and the adze. The stone was set in position with clay. Access to Dorset Hill was by way of a trail blazed through the forest for foot traffic only. With determination and courage they tackled the task of carving a home from the wilderness and making it possible to live off the land.

Because of the urgent and desperate need to provide their daily bread and basic needs, settlers had to toil from dawn to dusk. There were no mechanical aids at that time to help settlers develop and cultivate their land, and they could remove only the undergrowth vegetation and small timber to clear space for a garden. Crops for food were grown among fallen and standing timber. Farming tools were beaten into shape from pieces of discarded scrap metal. A bramble was used to rake in the seeds. The humble garden hoe was the most important piece of equipment for breaking up newly cleared land for growing crops.

The early settlers experienced difficult times due to unseasonal weather and crop failure, which could cause a grave shortage of food. Then they had to cook thistles, nettles, and gather watercress and dandelions for salads. The eye of the potato would be scooped out for planting, and the remainder cooked for the evening meal.

The land carried dense vegetation and tall timber such as Blue Gum, Swamp Gum and Stringy Bark. Understory vegetation included manfern, bracken fern, native willow, wattle, fire weed, dogwood and native pear trees. Wild life was abundant - the wallaby, wombat, kangaroo, possum and also the white cockatoos did much damage to crops and pastures.

The destructive Tasmanian Devil and Native Cat were most numerous. They had unfortunately a keen taste for poultry. The wallaby and kangaroo however, provided a good meal for many hungry families, and rugs were made from the skins, especially those of the black and grey possum. Treated with home made tanning, a mixture of wattle bark, and carefully stretched, they were used for bed covers and lap rugs.

Through countless centuries the land had become covered with deep layers of timber and vegetation. Only by continuous burning off was it possible to convert the land to pasture and farm produce. Huge quantities of big timber were reduced to ash. Bush was felled to dry, and burned off in the autumn. Grass seed was sown after the burn to benefit from the autumn rain. Each year saw an increase in the amount of cleared land.

At Dorset Hill the main activity was dairy produce - butter and cheese. They also produced beef, mutton, pork and bacon, wool, potatoes and small fruit including cherries. As land clearing proceeded, cultivation improved with the use of a team and plough. Hay for stock fodder was grown and stored for winter feed. A yearly cycle of farm production had begun.

6 horses and carts delivering milk to the Bream Creek Butter Factory.

As time passed the home was extended to accommodate a growing family. Rooms were added to the original split timber hut using pit-sawn timber, and galvanised iron sheets replaced the original wooden shingles. The inside was lined with boards and covered with hessian, which in turn was covered with newspaper and patterned wall paper.

Like all homes of the period, the fireplace was the focal point for evening gatherings. The spacious fireplace was used to air linen and to cook the meals. To enable heavy cooking pots to be hung and removed easily, a swinging arm with a hook at its end was fitted into the stonework. The inside of the fireplace was rendered with a dressing of white clay.

Proven recipes handed down over the years were used to make soap, cheese, butter, jams, sauces and pickles. Fresh fruit was preserved with sulphur. Flower gardening was a popular hobby, and the large garden, enclosed by a picket fence, included roses, pansies, violets, snowdrops and other bulbs. Also there were red and black currants, gooseberries and strawberries.

To Roast a Swan

Black Swans are a totally protected species, but this recipe can be used by substituting Turkey.

Stuffing
1/2 loaf stale bread   2 eggs
1/2 litre tepid water   Salt & pepper to taste
4 chopped or powdered sassafras or marjoram leaves.

Bread Sauce
1 large onion   Salt & pepper to taste
500g stale bread   750ml boiling milk

Having picked, drawn and singed the bird, stuff the breast with a stuffing made of stale bread soaked in tepid water, squeezed dry and mixed with 2 eggs, seasoning, and sassafras. Sew up the neck and truss carcass. Cover the breast with oiled paper to keep from scorching, roast until a fine brown. Baste well and when nearly done remove oiled paper so breast can brown. A good sized bird will take 1-1/2 to 2 hours. You will have plenty of good gravy in the pan.

Bread sauce was used as garnish. Boil the onion with pepper until soft, mix with bread soaked in boiling milk, add chunk of butter walnut size, add salt & sassafras to taste.

Kangaroo Stew

1 kg diced kangaroo   2 medium onions
1-1/2 litres water   30g dripping
50 ml vinegar   80g flour
Salt & pepper to taste

If you procure a young kangaroo, let it hang for a few days to age, cut off tail (boil in stock to make kangaroo tail soup), bone the carcass, boil bones for stock. Cut meat in 2.5cm cubes. Heat 2 tablespoons of dripping in pot on fire and cook peeled, sliced onion until golden brown. Sprinkle large tablespoon flour to brown also. Add 1 litre water and seasoning to form gravy. Dip meat pieces in vinegar and add to gravy. Draw the pan to side of fire and simmer gently 4 hours or until tender.

Christmas Day in the 1890's on the MAY QUEEN, up the Lune River.
Skipper: Jim Miley (facing camera), Crew: Joe Connors and Alf Nichols.
Menu included a pig's head and potatoes boiled in their skins.
Note the 'Tucker Box' in centre of picture.

Baked Fish

500 to 800g whole fish	greased paper

Fish Sauce

40g butter	40g flour
250ml milk	50ml cream
50g bread crumbs	

Choose a nice large fish such as perch or trumpeter. Scale,
clean, wrap well in greased paper. Place in baking dish, bake in
hot oven for 20 minutes. Remove paper, garnish with sauce
made by melting butter, and mixing with flour and half of milk
and juices from fish. Beat together, add rest of milk and cream.
Place fish on serving dish, pour sauce over and sprinkle toasted
bread crumbs.

Native Hen

I have yet to meet someone who has succeeded in achieving any degree of tenderness. The best advice I have had is to fill a pot with water, place in it 2 native hens and 2 river pebbles, bring to boil and simmer overnight. In the morning discard the hens and serve the pebbles.

Wild Duck

Stuffing

4 medium onions
250g bread crumbs
Salt & pepper to taste

4 sage leaves
60g butter

Game Sauce

200ml (1 cup) port wine
40g butter
Pinch nutmeg

Gravy from duck
40g flour
Salt & pepper to taste

Truss duck including the feet, which should be scalded and skin peeled off. To make stuffing, boil onions until quite tender, add sage, mix well with bread crumbs, half butter, and seasoning. Stuff and sew up neck and cavity, bake 1-1/2 hours. Serve with sauce made by simmering wine and gravy with nutmeg and seasoning. Melt rest of butter, mix to smooth paste with flour, stir in and simmer 5 minutes.

Scallops

I would not recommend this recipe as it produces flavourless bullets, but it is a good example of the gross overcooking of seafood.

250ml milk
40g butter

40g S.R. flour
Salt & pepper to taste

Take white & yellow from shell, wash well in cold then warm water. Put in saucepan with milk, simmer 1/2 hour, or until tender, and remove from milk. Make white sauce of flour, butter, & pepper melted and mixed in hot milk, beating well. Add scallops, serve on buttered toast.
My suggestion would be to make the sauce, thicken it further, put the raw scallops in and simmer for 5 minutes then serve.

Whitebait Fritters

300g Whitebait   150g S.R. flour
Salt & pepper to taste   50 ml milk
1 teaspoon baking powder   1 egg

Make a thick batter by mixing egg, flour, seasoning, and baking powder in milk. Add fish and put tablespoons full into hot lard to fry until golden brown, turning halfway.

Boiled Crayfish Salad

1 crayfish about 800g   150ml vinegar
100g salt   100g sugar

Drown crayfish in fresh water then plunge into boiling water with vinegar, salt, & sugar. Cook about 10 minutes per 400g, then plunge into cold water. Rub over with salad oil. Separate body from tail, split in half. Crack legs and arrange on serving dish.

Abalone

250g abalone   1 egg
60g bread crumbs   Salt & pepper to taste

Abalone were once plentiful along the shoreline and could be picked up close to shore by wading. As the usual method of tenderising (boiling for a long time) did not work, they were usually made into patties.

Mince the abalone flesh, mix with egg and bread crumbs, fry in boiling fat.

Potted Possum

700g possum minced   1 litre milk
100g minced fatty bacon or ham   80g bread crumbs
Salt & pepper to taste   Ground mace

Soak minced meat in cold milk 2 hours. Drain, add bacon, seasoning & mace. Press into straight sided jar, cover with brown paper, steam for 2 hours by standing in pot of boiling water, replenishing water as needed. When cooked, cool and turn out to serve cold.

The use of native fare declined for all but the very poor with the wider cultivation of conventional vegetables, poultry, sheep, pigs and cattle. However, circumstances still required minimum waste, and the use of all parts of their animals gave a large variety of dishes. Cooking facilities varied from wood ranges to dutch ovens suspended over the fire, and improvised camp ovens.

Roast Lamb Head & Pluck

1 onion	Parsley, salt & pepper to taste
25g flour	1 lamb's head, heart and 1/2 liver

After washing head, remove brains; put head, heart and 1/2 liver in pan and cover with water. Add salt and peeled onion, boil 1-1/4 hours. Remove head and brown in oven or stand before fire. Boil brains in pan liquor then mince with liver and heart; dredge with flour, parsley, salt & pepper, add enough water to make sauce thick as cream. Cook three minutes then pour over roasted head and serve.

Stewed Beef Kidney

1 large beef kidney	1 bayleaf
20g coarse salt	Salt & pepper to taste
20g butter or lard	1 onion, sliced
50g flour	

Wash kidney and stand 15 minutes in cold water. Place in pot with cold salt water and stew until tender. Remove and slice. Gently saute with salt, pepper, onion and butter; add flour and stir until quite thick. Best served for breakfast on hot buttered toast.

Brawn

1 pig's head and feet	Pepper, salt & nutmeg to taste

Clean and divide the head; put head, nose, ears and feet in saucepan with water to cover, simmer covered 4 to 5 hours until meat falls off bone. Strain and reserve reduced liquid. Remove all bones. Season and put into earthenware bowl; cover with reserved liquid and cool. Turn out to use.

Tripe in White Onion Sauce

1kg fresh tripe
1 kg onions
50g flour

1 litre milk
50g butter
Salt & pepper to taste

Clean tripe well. Cut in 2cm strips and boil in 1/2 litre milk and 1/2 litre water 45 minutes. Strain, smother with white onion sauce and serve.

White Onion Sauce

Peel and slice onions, boil in 1/2 litre milk until tender. Reserve liquid. Rub onion through sieve. Melt butter over low heat, then add flour and onion pulp, cook adding reserved milk until creamy texture.

Dormers

500g leftover cooked lamb/mutton
Pepper & salt to taste
100g breadcrumbs

50g beef suet
100g boiled rice
1 egg

Finely chop or mince meat & suet, add to rice with seasoning & egg to bind. Form patties and cover with breadcrumbs then fry in hot dripping until brown.

True Irish Stew

1 kg breast of mutton cut in pieces
1-1/2 kg potatoes cut in chunks
2 large onions, peeled, sliced

1-1/2 litres water
Salt & pepper to taste

Stew breast of mutton 1 hour in water, then drain off and reserve liquid. Alternate layers of potato with layers of meat, onion and seasoning in pot then pour reserved liquid over. Stew another hour, shaking well now and then to keep from sticking on the bottom.

Fried Ox Feet or Cow Heel

80g breadcrumbs
1 egg yolk
Parsley, cayenne, salt & pepper to taste

Wash, scald and thoroughly clean the foot meat. Cut into strips. Mix breadcrumbs with seasonings. Dip meat strips in egg yolk, then breadcrumbs, then fry in lard until brown.

Stewed Oxtail

1 oxtail	6 peppercorns
2 onions	1 blade mace
1 bay leaf	1 carrot
50g cooking oil	1 turnip
1/2 cup chopped parsley	50g flour
1 litre water or meat stock	Salt & pepper to taste

Cut tail into joints. Peel and slice onion. Heat fat in saucepan, fry pieces of tail; when brown remove and then fry onion, brown thoroughly. Drain off fat then return pieces of tail to pan and add 1 litre water or stock. Add seasonings, bring to boil and simmer 3 to 4 hours. Remove tail to a basin. Skim fat from liquid, re-heat and thicken with flour mixed to paste with some of the skimmed fat. Add tail and vegetables cut in strips; simmer until well cooked; serve on dish and garnish with vegetables.

Steak and Kidney Pudding

500g lean beef	2 sheep kidneys
1/2 cup chopped parsley	40g flour
Salt & pepper to taste	1/2 litre water
200g suet crust*	

Cut meat into cubes. Skin and wash kidneys then slice. Mix meat and kidney slices with flour and seasonings. Make suet crust.* Cut off 1/3 for top then knead remainder and roll out thinly; line a greased pudding basin. Add meat mixture and add 1/2 litre water. Cover with rest of pastry and pinch edges together. Cover with pudding cloth and tie with string to keep in place. Place carefully in large pan of boiling water, leaving top exposed. Boil 2 hours, then remove and serve.

*Suet Crust

200g flour	Pinch baking soda
80g finely minced suet	Salt
Water to mix	

Mix dry ingredients, add water and knead on floured surface. Roll out to size and shape required.

Suet crust is suitable for all boiled puddings.

Dec 1925 Early morning leaving to go fruit picking

To Roast a Rabbit

2 young rabbits	25g suet chopped finely
50g breadcrumbs	10g lemon peel, grated
1 egg	Pinch thyme, marjoram, savoury
25g flour	Salt & pepper to taste
100ml water	Melted butter or dripping to baste
25g butter	String and large needle

Having drawn and skinned the rabbits, wash in warm water then dry and stuff with mixture of breadcrumbs, suet, lemon peel, spices and egg. Truss with string and sew up. Bake slowly in oven 100°c, 1-1/2 hours, basting frequently with butter or dripping. When cooked, place in serving dish. Melt butter, add flour to make paste, add water into pan juice and thicken with butter/ flour paste; pour over rabbits and serve.

Moulded Fowl

1 fowl or any game bird	1 large carrot
1 onion	6 peppercorns
1 blade mace	1 white turnip
20g gelatine	2 egg whites
Salt & pepper to taste	1-1/2 litres water

Roughly cut up fowl and vegetables. Include seasonings and simmer in water 1-1/2 hours. Remove fowl from pan and strip out bones; return bones to pan and boil further 1-1/2 hours. Strain, add gelatine to liquid, whisk in egg whites to clear mixture. Strain and put a little into greased mould; cut meat in strips and decorate around mould; fill up with meat and cooling jelly. Allow to set; turn out when cold and serve.

Dresden Patties

1/2 cold cooked fowl	50g cooked ham
1 litre stock or water	700g cream
Juice 1 lemon	40g flour
Cayenne pepper	40g butter
1 loaf stale bread	1 egg, beaten
Salt & pepper to taste	100g breadcrumbs

Cut bread in 5cm slices, leave crust on. Use scone cutter or the like to cut halfway into each slice and remove centre, leaving a depression. Dip slices in cream, drain then brush beaten egg all over, dust with breadcrumbs and fry in hot fat until brown both sides. Drain then fill with chicken mixture prepared as follows.

Dice chicken and ham finely. Melt butter in pan and mix flour in to make paste; add stock and stir until it thickens, then add 60ml cream and seasonings. Add meat and heat thoroughly,

Fish Baked in Vinegar

1 kg filleted fish, cubed	150ml vinegar
Salt, pepper, nutmeg, allspice to taste	

Stack fish in earthenware jar; mix seasoning with vinegar and pour over. Tie brown paper over top of jar and prick with fork. Bake in slow oven and serve cold. Keeps well.

Yorkshire Pudding

Usually served with roast beef, but is good with
all meat and poultry dishes

250g flour, sifted   2 eggs, beaten
750ml milk   Pinch salt

Place flour in basin, make well and add salt and eggs, then add milk slowly while stirring to moisten all flour. Beat well, adding remaining milk and stand 30 minutes.Grease square tin, heat until hot then pour in batter and bake 45 minutes. Serve in neatly cut squares.

Blackjack

(Parisian Essence, Colouring Caramel)

250g sugar   50ml and 250ml water

Put sugar and 50ml water in pan over heat and stir well until sugar is dark brown (not black and burnt). Add 250ml water, stir well, cool and bottle. Add to stews and sauces to give a richer colour. It will not add to or enhance the flavour - only the appearance.

Boiled Tongue

Steep 1 beef tongue in cold water overnight, then wash thoroughly in morning. Boil /simmer 2 to 3 hours, skimming the surface occasionally. Serve cold or hot.

Baked Fish

(River Trout, Cod or any moderate sized fish)
Wrap fish in buttered greaseproof paper, place in baking dish and cook in hot oven 20 minutes. Can be garnished with a sauce or served with lemon.

Kedgeree of Fish

100g cooked rice   500g cold steamed fish
50g butter   Salt & pepper to taste
2 eggs, hard boiled

Melt butter in stewpan, add rice, seasoning and fish; heat through. Pile it high on a dish and garnish with sliced hard boiled egg.

Sassafras Beer

Sassafras is a sub-alpine rainforest timber. Its bark and leaves taste of pepper, allspice and cloves.

20 litres water
125g ginger (powdered or crushed)
25g brewers yeast

125g hops
250g sassafras bark

Add hops, ginger and bark to water, boil 1 hour. When lukewarm strain through jelly bag and put in cask or fermenter, while still slightly warm stir in yeast. Let stand 3 days, skim each day. Strain into bottles and seal. Ready in 3 weeks.

Clearing land by hand was heavy work that used a lot of energy.

Fish Roe on Toast

100g roe   100g cream
Juice of 1 lemon   1 egg, beaten
Cayenne, salt & pepper to taste

Wash roe, put in basin with cream, lemon and seasoning, then add beaten egg. Cook in saucepan over heat and stir until hot and thick. Spread on buttered toast and serve hot.

Vegetables

Because some vegetables can be stored for long periods, with only gradual deterioration, they were used widely by our forbears; it was unusual to see less than three veg and often five or six were served with a meal. To test if cooked, pass a fork through the stalks of cabbages, cauliflowers, etc. All greens used to be boiled with plenty of water and salt, the water boiling when they were put in, and kept boiling and with a very small amount of bicarb soda to mellow the greens and preserve their colour. It is now widely believed that bicarb soda destroys vitamin C, and colour is preserved by steam cooking without immersing in water.

Beetroot

Wash carefully without breaking tops and boil in salted water 1/2 to 1 hour according to age and size. Drain and cover with cold water to loosen skins, which should rub off. Serve hot or chill, slice, and serve with salad.

Cauliflower

Remove coarse outside leaves and stalk, leaving the smaller leaves that curl into the flower. Wash and soak in salted water for 1/2 hour. Drain and put in large saucepan of boiling salted water, with the flower turned down. Simmer gently until tender. Lift and drain, place in a round vegetable dish, flower up. Mask with hot melted butter sauce and serve.

Cabbage

Remove outside leaves, cut into quarters and remove stalk. Wash and soak in salted water. Drain then cook as a green vegetable. Lift into colander and press all water out, using a plate. Place in hot vegetable dish, cut across and across; add butter and pepper, and serve.

Broad Beans

Shell and drop in boiling water; simmer until skins begin to break. Drain and serve in hot vegetable dish with melted butter poured over.

Celery

Separate stalks and cut into 10cm sticks. Wash well and treat as for cauliflower.

French Beans

Wash the beans carefully and remove ends and strings. Put into boiling salted water and boil rapidly until beans are tender. Drain in colander. Return to saucepan with knob of butter and shake over the fire. If beans are old, a pinch of bicarbonate of soda will tenderise them while boiling.

Boiled Potatoes

Potatoes should be as near the same size as possible, or the small ones will break before the large ones are done. Put them in cold water with a lump of salt, and bring to the boil slowly. When they begin to crack pour off the water and set the saucepan a little off the fire until they are quite dry and mealy.

Lentils

Wash well and boil gently for 1 to 1-1/2 hours in enough water to cover them. A little dripping, salt and pepper in the water adds flavour. They should be kept carefully stirred. Serve hot.

Spinach

Spinach should be well washed, the veins and stalks removed, and leaves cooked with very little water. Add salt and cook till tender; drain and chop finely. Return to pan with a little butter, reheat and serve hot.

Vegetable Marrow

Cut into convenient sized pieces, peel thinly and remove seeds. Cook as for cauliflower, sprinkle finely chopped parsley over and serve.

Carrots, Turnips and Swedes

Wash and peel, cut into rings or slice and cook in salted water until tender. Drain and toss with a little honey. Serve hot.

Candied Lemon Peel

500g sugar to 200ml water

Cut lemons in quarters removing flesh with spoon to leave only peel. Cover with salted water, soak 7 days. Put in fresh water, simmer 2 hours. Make up enough syrup to cover peel and boil 10 minutes. Drain peel, add syrup, simmer 30 minutes. Drain peel and put in warm place to dry.

Marmalade

6 oranges	6 lemons
5kg sugar	5 litres water

Peel lemons thinly, shred rind. Cut up oranges and lemon fruit finely, removing pith and seeds. Place in 5 litres water and leave overnight. In morning, add lemon rind and boil quickly about 1 hour without sugar; then add sugar and boil 40 minutes and bottle. It looks thin but will soon gel.

Quince Jelly

To every 500g fruit add 750ml water

Boil water and fruit until fruit begins to break. Strain through cheesecloth 1 hour without applying any pressure. Simmer resulting juice 1/2 hour. To each 750ml juice add 500g sugar and boil until it gels, then bottle.

Grape Jelly

Wash grapes and remove stems. Place in preserving pan and mash until broken. Heat slowly and cook until juice is well drawn out. Drain through cheese cloth for 1 hour applying no pressure. Measure resulting juice and add an equal volume of sugar; boil together 15 minutes then skim and strain again. Boil again until surface looks wrinkled and liquid gels on edges of pan. Fill jars while hot.

Pickled Onions

Select small pickling onions; peel then steep in strong salt water 4 days, changing water twice. Drain and allow to dry, then place in boiling milk few minutes. Allow to cool then wash and allow to dry. Put in jars and fill with white wine, vinegar or malt vinegar with a few cloves. Seal and store at least 1 month before using.

Tomato Sauce

6kg tomatoes
30g garlic
1 tablespoon allspice
15g chilli powder
15 cloves
1.5 litres vinegar

500g apples
500g onions
500g sugar
15g mace
30g curry powder

Break tomatoes, peel and slice onions & apples then cut finely with garlic. Add all other ingredients and boil 3 hours. Strain, push through coarse sieve then bottle.

Apple Chutney

10 large cooking apples
5 large onions, peeled, sliced
1 tablespoon dry English mustard
10g ground black pepper

1kg dark sugar
1.5 litres vinegar
1 teaspoon salt
10g cayenne

Peel, core and slice apples. Mix all together; boil 3 hours then bottle in sterilised jars and seal.

Clear Green Tomato Pickle

5kg green tomatoes
10g whole spice
10g mace
1.5 litres vinegar

900g sugar
30g peppercorn
10g cloves

Make brine (in 1 litre water dissolve 2 tablespoons salt).
Slice green tomatoes and stand in brine 24 hours then strain.
Boil the vinegar, sugar, spice, mace, pepper and cloves, add the
tomatoes and boil until clear and tender, then bottle.

Pickled Red Cabbage or Cauliflower

Take 1 good sized cabbage, peel off straggly leaves and
slice thinly into bowl. Sprinkle salt over and leave in cool place
48 hours. Drain off salt liquor which has formed. Boil vinegar.
Place cabbage in jars, pour vinegar over and seal. Cauliflower
should be cooked in boiling water until tender before putting in
vinegar.

Pickled Walnuts

Make strong brine by dissolving 2/3 cup salt in 1 litre water.
Gather green walnuts on New Years Day. Prick them all over with
fine skewer, then steep in strong brine 7 days. Dry until they turn
black, usually 2-3 days, then arrange in bottles. Boil enough
vinegar, seasoned with ginger & salt, to cover walnuts. Stand
until cold then cover. Ready in about 4 weeks.

The art of preserving food is extremely ancient, but only in the
nineteenth century did it move out of the home into industry. Prehistoric
curing was by drying, then with fire came smoking. This process
assisted by preliminary salting is still used today for such products as
ham and bacon. Placing fish and meat in barrels between layers of salt
was another method often used on sea voyages.

Canned foods became available after the can was invented in the
mid 1800's. Imagine being in an isolated settlement in mid winter, and
the joy of opening a can of peaches!

To Cure a Ham

8kg ham
60g saltpetre
30g black pepper

500g sea salt
250g common salt
750g treacle

Powder salt well; lay ham in mixture of dry ingredients for
about 4 days, turning and rubbing every day, then pour treacle
over and rub and turn each day for 28 days. Then soak in water
for 24 hours and hang to dry. It may then be boiled, baked, or
cold smoked.

Pickle for Beef

200g sea salt
2kg brown sugar
30g black pepper

100g saltpetre
500g common salt

Mix all ingredients and rub over beef. Turn, and rub in mixture, every day for three weeks. It may then be boiled, baked or cold smoked.

Good Household Soap

2.5kg fat (free from salt)
500g caustic soda
2.5 litres water

500g resin
250g borax

Put all ingredients in large pan, bring slowly to boil to dissolve resin. Watch carefully: if it rises to top of pan throw in a little cold water. Simmer gently 3 hours. When ready, soap will look stringy. Stir frequently when cooling. Pour into tin or moulds; when quite firm turn out and cut in bars.

Pickled Eggs

4 dozen eggs
15g ginger
6 cloves

750ml vinegar
1 teaspoon allspice

Boil eggs; cool in cold water, then peel. Arrange carefully in large mouth jars. Boil vinegar, allspice, ginger and cloves until all the flavour is extracted; strain and pour over eggs then seal.

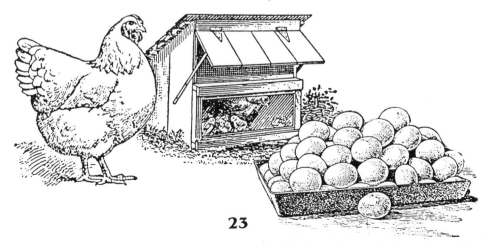

Shovel and Steamboat Cooking

A shovel or plowshare over the fire preceded the modern barbecue by centuries, and for quick cooking on the move was only rivalled by a green stick skewer. Suitable for grilling eggs, meat, pancakes etc. a shovel with a little lard is superb for shallow frying.

The river and coastal steamers provided the first regular, reliable transport for many settlers. They had fires in their boilers; even when moored the fires were kept going, damped down. A steel shovel was used as a baking tray for bread, roasts and vegetables, or in the morning for eggs, bacon, chops etc. While under way they tended to eat stews, sandwiches and soups.

Shovel Fritters

1 egg	Pinch salt
1 cup flour	1 teaspoon baking powder
1/4 cup milk or water	Knob butter or lard
Left over meat, poultry, vegetables, finely diced.	

Mix ingredients into thick batter. Clean face of shovel and heat over fire. Melt knob of butter or lard in cup of shovel and cook spoonfuls mixture 4 minutes each side or until cooked. Be careful not to put shovel too far into fire, or handle will burn!

Bush Rissoles

250g finely chopped possum, wallaby, beef, lamb, pork wild bird (or anything else that walks by)   1 egg
  1/2 cup flour   1 small onion
  1/2 cup breadcrumbs or soaked & squeezed bread

Mix ingredients and shape into patties. Heat some lard on the shovel and fry until cooked. Slices of potato can be fried after to accompany rissoles.

Continual Stew Stock Pot

When droving stock, timber cutting, or under way on a sail or steam boat, people needed hot nourishing food at odd hours of the day and night. A large stock pot was used continually. At least every 7 days it was finished, cleaned out and started again. Anything and everything was put in it, with the exception of onions, which induced fermentation, and flour which made it stick on the bottom. It was only a matter of adding more meat and vegetables every day. To make dishes with curry or onions, the amount required was removed to another pot over the fire, the flavouring and flour to thicken added, and served.

Bread Making
Bread is the Staff of Life

Bread has always played an important part in Australian fare. Much has been made of Damper as a part of the colonial diet; because of its speed of preparation and easy cooking by basic methods it was used when 'on the move.' As soon as roots were put down and the camp oven built, baking was a high priority. Wheat was ground into flour at local mills for a percentage of the product. Flour was easily transported, and kept dry it lasts very well. Yeasts were maintained and passed on through families.

Larger settlements attracted bakeries, but remote farms baked bread every two days until the 1950's, when factory produced bread and bulk transportation made bought bread more convenient. This gradually drove all but the most tenacious small bakeries out of business. Recent years have seen more small bakeries, and the re-commissioning of wood-fired ovens in old bakeries, supplying a trendy market.

Yeast

40g hops	2 medium potatoes
1 cup flour	60g sugar

Boil hops, potatoes in 2 litres water 20 minutes; strain and add sugar. When cool mix the flour with a little of the liquor, add rest of liquor and bottle in a flagon. Cork well. Use the same bottle, with a little of previous batch left in to make more. Over time, the yeast will get better and better. Maintain room temperature for yeast to mature in 8-10 hours.

Bread

3 kg flour, approx.	6 teaspoons sugar
3/4 cup yeast	2 teaspoons salt

Put flour in large bowl; make well in centre, pour in yeast, add 1 cup warm water and mix into batter. Cover well with flour then stand in warm place overnight. In morning, sprinkle salt on flour and add enough warm water to mix into a light dough. Cover with cloth and stand in warm place until doubled. Knead 5 minutes to give even elastic texture, then form into rolls/loaves, remembering that they will about triple in size. Leave 1 hour to rise again, then place in very hot oven 230°c, 10 minutes or until uniform golden brown. Decrease heat to 180°c; when cooked, a tap with finger will produce hollow sound.

Flour

Different flours, using the same methods and yeast, produce different results.

Plain White Flour (wheat flour)

The colour, texture and nutrition depend on the degree of milling and refining. Most white flour today is highly refined and low in nutrition and taste.

Wholemeal

Ground from whole grain, grain endosperm and husk. Makes dark, chewy, strongly flavoured and close textured bread.

Rye

On its own or mixed with white flour, gives a sharp flavour and fine texture. Keeps well.

Millers' Bread

Use the same method and quantities as for Bread, but add 3 teaspoons honey with 40g melted butter in first batter, and use wholemeal or stoneground flour.

Yeast Fruit Loaf

2 tablespoons brown sugar
2 cups plain white flour
100g sultanas
2 teaspoons candied peel
4 teaspoons allspice
Pinch salt
1/2 cup yeast or 6 teaspoons dried yeast

350ml lukewarm milk
1-3/4 cups wholemeal flour
75g currants
50g butter, melted
1 egg

Dissolve a little sugar in the warm milk; add yeast and leave 10 minutes or until frothy. Rub butter into flour then add fruit, sugar, salt, allspice; mix well. Whisk egg. Make well in flour, add egg and enough yeast-milk to make soft dough. Cover and leave in warm place to rise. Knead 5 minutes, place in warm greased tin; leave to rise in warm place 30 minutes. Bake in hot oven 200°c 20 minutes, then reduce to 160°c 30 minutes or until firm, brown, and slightly shrunken from sides of tin. Brush top with honey to glaze.

Desserts, Confectionery and Cakes

Desserts have been an important part of people's fare since early settlement. When other things have been in seasonal short supply, there were always flour, sugar and eggs. Desserts were made of dry goods, preserved fruits and canned fruit. Dining out as we know it was rare, but afternoon tea parties were elaborate prestigious events where one was judged on the quality of the baking, napery and crockery. Suppers at Balls and other night events were grand, with each woman contributor having a special dish that was renowned.

Baking cakes and biscuits for the home was a weekly or sometimes daily event. Plain and fruit cakes were provided for morning and afteroon tea for workmen, and the lunch known as Dinner was the large hot meal of the day. Most people worked from home or close to it.

Confectionery was made at home, and provided the sugar boost needed with hard manual labour. Bought lollies were a rare luxury. Most children helped make lollies as they had a vested interest.

Afternoon Tea Cakes

500g flour	150g butter
100g sugar	Pinch salt
250ml milk	100g jam
2 eggs, beaten	
1-1/2 teaspoons cream of tartar	

Rub butter and sugar into flour then add jam, eggs and milk. Mix well. Roll small portions of dough into marbles and bake on greased slide in hot oven 200°c 15-20 minutes or until light golden brown.

Apple Cake

250g S.R. flour	70g sugar
100ml milk	1 egg
40g butter	150g stewed apples

Mix well all ingredients except apples, to form dough. Roll out 3-5mm thick. Cut in half; spread apple on one half, top with other half, seal edges. Prick top with fork, brush with milk, sprinkle little castor sugar. Bake on greased slide in oven 200°c until light golden brown.

The parlour, furnished with treasures and family bible brought from
'The old country,' and the washroom, with the bath hanging on the wall.

'Afternoon Tea' Scones

500g S.R. flour   80g butter
200ml milk   Sugar to taste

Mix all ingredients well, adding enough milk to make firm dough. Roll out 15mm thick, cut with scone cutter or can opened at both ends. Bake on greased tray 200°c, 15-20 minutes or until risen with firm brown crust.

Drop Scones

200g plain flour   100g sugar
1 teaspoon baking soda   3 eggs, well beaten
100ml milk

Sieve flour then mix all dry ingredients in bowl; make well, add eggs and enough milk to make firm batter. Mix well. Drop tablespoonsful on hot, greased pan; as soon as they bubble turn with slice. Cool quickly.

Aunty's Patty Cakes

100g butter   100g sugar
100g cornflour   100g plain flour
Lemon essence to taste   2 eggs, well beaten
25g dessicated coconut   100ml milk
1 teaspoon baking powder

Cream butter and sugar in bowl, add eggs, then all other ingredients. Mix to thick batter. Put tablespoonfulls in patty cake tins and bake in hot oven 5-10 minutes.

Shortbread

1kg flour, sifted   200g ground rice or rice flour
700g butter   250g sugar
2 teaspoons baking powder

Soften butter and knead in sugar with enough flour to give heavy consistency. Roll out 10mm thick, place on greased baking tray, mark out into fingers with knife. Prick each finger at least 4 times then bake in moderate oven 160°c, 30 minutes or until golden brown.

Gingerbread

500g flour
150g treacle
150g butter
1 teaspoon cinnamon
1 tablespoon powdered ginger

250g sugar
200ml boiling water
1 egg, beaten
Pinch salt
10g baking soda

Mix well sugar, treacle and butter, add egg then spices, baking soda and salt. Add flour gradually, moistening with hot water. Roll flat and place on greased baking tray. Mark with knife so it breaks in regular pieces when cooked, or cut out gingerbread figures, and bake 170°c, 30 minutes. Decorate with icing.

Treacle Sponge

250g flour
150g treacle
1 egg
Nutmeg to taste

150g suet
100ml milk
60g sugar

Mix all the ingredients to a batter and pour into a buttered pudding basin. Cover and steam or boil for 1-1/2 hours.

Iced Cinnamon Cake

100g sugar
50g butter
100ml milk
200g plain flour

2 eggs
1 teaspoon cinnamon
1 teaspoon baking powder

Preheat oven 180°c. Cream butter and sugar, add eggs one by one, beating well. Sieve flour with baking powder & cinnamon and add to mixture alternately with milk. Bake in greased cake tin lined with greased paper or baking paper, 180°c, 35-45 minutes. When cooked, a depression made by lightly touching surface will spring back.

ICING:

150ml milk   150g brown sugar   40g butter

Bring milk & sugar to boil in large pan, stirring until sugar dissolved. Turn down heat to keep mixture just boiling and cook without stirring 1/2 hour. Remove from heat, add butter and beat until it cools and begins to set. Spread smoothly over cake.

Sponge Cake

The texture of a sponge depends on the beating of air into the eggs. Castor sugar should always be used. Tins should be lightly greased then floured; sponges should be baked as soon as mixed. Usually when cooked there is shrinkage around the edge of the tin, and when pressed on the top, the depressed surface should spring back.

2 eggs, separated	100g castor sugar
100g S.R. flour	20g butter
Pinch salt	1/4 cup hot water

Beat egg whites until stiff, add sugar gradually, beating until thick; add yolks. Sift flour & salt then fold into egg mixture. Lightly, evenly fold in melted butter & water quickly and lightly pour into sponge tin and bake at 180°c 20 minutes; turn out on wire rack.

Albert Pudding

100g rice	750ml milk
150g raisins	lemon peel & cinnamon to taste
100g sugar	3 eggs, beaten

Heat milk with lemon, cinnamon and sugar until small bubbles appear on side of pan. Remove from heat; stir some warm milk into beaten eggs. Blend egg mixture into milk mixture, stirring rapidly. Return to heat and cook until mixture coats a metal spoon. Do not over cook. Add rice which has been rinsed, then place in buttered casserole dish. Place dish in pan of hot water and oven bake uncovered 160°c, 2-1/2 hours. Add raisins after first hour, and stir to distribute rice.

Jam or Golden Syrup Pudding

500g flour	200g suet
100g jam or syrup	1 teaspoon baking soda
100ml milk	

Put jam or golden syrup in bottom of pudding basin. Mix flour, suet and baking soda with milk to make a thick batter then pour over jam. Cover basin and steam or boil about 1-1/2 hours. Keep up water level by adding boiling water as needed. Turn out upside down with the jam running over the cake.

Apple Charlotte

12 apples, peeled, cored, sliced
1/2 loaf of bread
Essence of lemon to taste
60g breadcrumbs
Juice 1 lemon
50g butter
100g sugar
Cream, whipped

Line pie dish with slices of buttered bread moistened with water, sugar and lemon. Layer apple slices in dish; sprinkle sugar and lemon juice over. Put layer of breadcrumbs over. Sprinkle rest of sugar; melt butter and pour over breadcrumbs. Bake in moderate oven 160°c - 180°c 1 hour. Cool, serve with whipped cream.

Gooseberry Fool

1 kg gooseberries
Sugar to taste
Nutmeg to taste
Whipped cream
750ml water
2 eggs, separated
750ml milk

Boil gooseberries in water until soft. Strain, sweeten and cool. Put milk and beaten egg yolks in pan and stir over hot water until mixture thickens. Remove from heat, cool. Swirl gooseberry puree through. Beat egg whites until stiff; fold through gooseberry mixture gently. Spoon into wine glasses, top with sweetened whipped cream.

Cream Puffs

60g butter
300ml water
115g flour
3 eggs

Boil water and butter; stir in flour all at once; beat well over heat until smooth and cooked enough to clear sides of pan. Allow to cool. Add eggs one at a time, beating well after each. Drop dessertspoonsful on greased oven slide; bake 30 minutes, 200°c without opening oven. When removed, prick with point of sharp knife to release steam. Cool, open tops, fill with cream.

Trifle

Port or sherry if liked
350ml whipped cream
4 bananas or fresh or canned fruit
13 cm square plain cake, bit stale
750ml custard, warm, thick

Slice cake, put some in dish. Sprinkle port or sherry if desired, then layer of fruit, then custard over top; then repeat layers until all used. Chill then top with whipped cream before serving.

Blancmange

15g arrowroot

1 litre milk

3 lemon tree leaves or rind 1/2 lemon

Sugar to taste

Mix arrowroot with 350ml milk, put other 650ml milk on heat with lemon leaves or lemon rind (or sometimes a few peach leaves which give almond flavour). Steep until flavoured; strain and return to heat; add sugar and arrowroot milk while stirring. When thickened pour into mould(s), chill and serve with stewed fruit or jam.

Raspberry Cream

1 kg fresh raspberries

15g gelatine, melted in little water

1-1/2 litres cream

Grated rind & juice 1 lemon

60g castor sugar

Blend raspberries, add lemon juice & rind, beat well. Add sugar to cream, beating lightly. Add raspberries to cream gradually; add gelatine. Whisk briskly until stiff, and serve.

In 1929, local families pooled their labour to pick raspberries.

Christmas Mince for mince pies

300g best suet	500g currants
200g candied peel	500g raisins
500g sugar	500g apples
1 tablespoon nutmeg	Peel 1 lemon, grated
10g allspice	

Peel, core and finely dice apple. Mince suet, chop candied peel. Combine all ingredients mixing well; put in stone jar and press down to exclude air. Tie on cover of brown paper soaked in brandy. Leave few days before using.

Christmas Pudding

(Made in October or November)

500g butter	500g sugar
8 eggs	200g breadcrumbs, sifted
500g flour	1 tablespoon carb. soda
10g cinnamon	10g allspice
2 teaspoons nutmeg	500g currants
500g raisins	500g sultanas
60g almonds	200g chopped dates
100g candied peel	4 tablespoons brandy
1 orange	

Cream butter & sugar, add eggs one at a time, beating well after each. Stir in flour and fruit, then add other ingredients; stir thoroughly. Place in clean pudding cloth and boil 8 hours. Hang in dry place until needed, then boil 2 hours and serve.

Christmas Cake

1.25kg flour	250g butter
250ml cream	250g treacle
250g brown sugar	2 eggs, whisked
15g powdered ginger	250g raisins
10g bicarb. soda	

Chop up raisins; sift flour, warm butter. Put flour in basin, mix in sugar, ginger, raisins; when well mixed, stir in butter, treacle, eggs. Beat mixture 10 minutes then mix bicarb evenly through dough. Butter cake tin or mould and pour in mixture. Bake 1-3/4 to 2 hours, 190°c.

Just as most entertainment had to be home made, so were the lollies. Many sweets popular years ago are seldom seen now.

French Jellies

Soak one packet gelatine in a cup of cold water overnight, put in saucepan with 1kg sugar & 1/2 cup hot water; boil 15 minutes. Flavour (e.g. 2 teaspoons lemon juice), pour into soup plates (wet plates with cold water first). When set cut into squares, and roll in icing sugar.

Baker's Toast
(Similar to honeycomb)

4 tablespoons sugar   2 tablespoons golden syrup

Boil in saucepan 7 minutes, stirring frequently. Add 1 teaspoon carb. soda, stir quickly and pour into buttered dish.

Coconut Ice

4 cups sugar   1 cup milk
1 cup coconut   Colouring

Prepare a wetted dish. Boil milk & sugar 10 minutes, stirring all time. Remove from heat, add coconut, beat until stiff. Pour half into dish, colour remainder with cochineal and pour over the white, spread with knife.

Marshmallows

1/3 cup gelatine   1kg sugar
1-1/2 cups boiling water   1 cup cold water
Vanilla to taste

Soak gelatine in cold water; bring other ingredients to boil and add soaked gelatine. Boil 20 minutes, then put in large basin. Cool slightly and flavour. Beat until thick, pour into swiss roll tin, sprinkle thickly with icing sugar. Cut in squares when cold.

Chocolate Almonds

Blanched almonds   Coating chocolate

Bake almonds in gentle oven until slightly coloured. Prepare coating chocolate, dip almonds one at a time, and place to dry.

Caramel Toffee

125g butter   250g brown sugar
Small tin sweetened condensed milk   Vanilla essence

Prepare well greased shallow tin. Melt butter in saucepan, add condensed milk and mix well. Flavour with few drops vanilla and add brown sugar, stirring with wooden spoon until melted, then bring to boil and cook rapidly five minutes, stirring often. Pour into tin and cut in squares just before it sets, using sharp knife.

Marshmallow Cones

1 cup white sugar   1 dessertspoon gelatine
3/4 cup cold water   Vanilla essence
Hundreds & thousands

Boil ingredients together three minutes then cool. Add essence and beat until thick. Spoon into ice cream cones and sprinkle with hundreds & thousands. Makes 10 cones.

Russian Caramels

125g butter   1 tin condensed milk
250g brown sugar   2 tablespoons golden syrup

Melt butter & other ingredients in saucepan. Stir over low heat until dark brown and mixture leaves sides of pan. Pour in greased tin. When cold cut in squares.

Peanut Brittle

500g salted peanuts   3/4 cup sugar
65g butter

Mix ingredients in frying pan 180°C stirring for 10 - 15 minutes. Add 2 teaspoons vanilla. Spread on sheet of foil and sprinkle with salt. When cool, break into pieces.

Chocolate Toffee

1 tin sweetened condensed milk   60g butter
125g dark chocolate   500g brown sugar

Melt butter, add sugar, stir until dissolved. Boil few minutes, add chocolate, when well mixed add condensed milk; cook gently but do not boil. Turn into buttered tin to cool.

Rice Bubbles & Date Fingers

3/4 cup dates, chopped   1/2 cup melted butter
1/2 cup sugar   3 cups rice bubbles
2 tablespoons coconut

Mix sugar, dates & butter; bring to boil, stirring all time. Remove from heat, pour over rice bubbles & coconut, mix thoroughly. Spread in shallow tin and press firmly. Sprinkle coconut over and cool. Cut in fingers, store in refrigerator.

Turkish Delight

2 tablespoons gelatine   1-1/4 cups water
2 cups sugar   1/2 teaspoon tartaric acid
12 drops essence

Soak gelatine in water until swollen. Put in saucepan with sugar, tartaric acid, and essence; boil ten minutes. Pour into buttered dish. When cold cut into shapes and roll in icing sugar, or hundreds & thousands.

The Fifties saw big changes in ways of living and eating. American influence was strong, and grew through the sixties and seventies - and not just in the fast food area.

The large influx of migrants and refugees brought many more changes. Italians were used to pasta and seafood; they encouranged us to use more squid, octopus and shellfish. From Germany, Hiungary, Switzerland and others, came processed foods; smoked and cured sausage and meats. From the Nordic countries came smorgasbord and smoked salmon.

The Spanish, Portuguese, Greeks and many others influenced what Australian people ate by opening restaurants and food shops. Many beautiful dishes were altered to cater for the perceived Australian taste, so even then we were adapting dishes to suit our local produce. Quite often it only needed chilli to be served as Spanish, tomato to be Italian, and cream to be French.

HANG YOUR HERBS
SOMEWHERE DRY
AND SHADY

Tuna Macaroni

3 medium tomatoes, chopped   500g tinned tuna
1 x 300g tin cream mushroom soup 100ml milk
200g grated cheese   2 cups macaroni
Tobasco sauce to taste

Cook macaroni in boiling salted water until just tender, wash well. Mix tomatoes with macaroni, soup, milk, tuna and sauce. Pour into greased baking dish, sprinkle cheese generously; bake 30 minutes.

Beef A La Mode

375g tin Camp Pie, diced   2 teaspoons cornflour
375g tin tomatoes   Bicarb soda
150g tin carrots   Salt and pepper to taste

Drain liquid from carrots & tomatoes into saucepan. Bring to boil, thicken with little cornflour and simmer few minutes. Add meat, tomato & carrots, heat well. Add pinch bicarb soda, salt & pepper. Serve sauce around the meat.

Lobster Thermidor

A very popular restaurant dish of the day.
1 X 800g lobster (crayfish)   250ml milk
Tablespoon tomato paste   25g butter
Dash tobasco to taste   25g flour
Salt & pepper to taste   200g cream
20g Gruyere cheese   25ml brandy
Sprinkle of paprika   Mashed potato

Cut lobster in halves lengthwise. Break legs & head, retrieve meat - this with tail meat should be roughly diced. Heat milk. In another pan melt butter, add flour, cook few minutes without browning. Add milk, tomato, salt, sugar, tobasco. Simmer whilst stirring for about 5 minutes then stir in lobster meat, cream & brandy; keep.hot but do not boil.

Mash potato and pipe some on the plate to place the tail shell on, then pipe rest around shell. Fill shell with thermidor mixture and sprinkle cheese & paprika on top. Brown potato and thermidor under grill. Serves 2.

Spaghetti Bolognaise

350g spaghetti	4 sprigs parsley, chopped
250g fine mince	1 teaspoon dried mixed herbs
10ml olive oil	150g tin tomato paste
50 ml red wine	1 onion finely chopped
100ml water	2 cloves garlic chopped
2 medium tomatoes, peeled, chopped	

Heat oil in frying pan, add onions & garlic, cook until transparent. Add mince, cook 10 minutes. Add tomato, parsley, tomato paste, and lastly red wine & water. Cover pan, simmer 45 minutes. Boil spaghetti briskly in salted water until tender. Drain and place on individual serving dishes. Spoon generous serve of sauce over and sprinkle cheese & parsley. Serves 4.

Chicken Maryland

4 chicken breasts with wing on to the first joint

100g seasoned flour	100g breadcrumbs
40g butter	200ml cooking oil
1 egg	50ml milk

Corn Fritters

1 teaspoon baking powder	100g plain flour
1 egg, separated	50ml milk
100g frozen/tinned corn kernels	Salt & pepper to taste

Fried Bananas

4 bananas	50g breadcrumbs	1 egg

Beat egg into milk. Roll chicken breasts in seasoned flour then egg mixture; coat with breadcrumbs. Heat butter & oil and saute chicken both sides until golden brown; place in casserole dish and bake in moderate oven 30 minutes or until cooked. Serve with fried banana and corn fritters.

Bananas

Cut bananas in half lengthwise, dip in egg and roll in breadcrumbs. Fry in oil till golden brown on both sides.

Fritters

Sift flour with baking powder, salt & pepper. Beat egg yolk with milk, add corn and mix thoroughly with flour mixture. Beat egg white until stiff, and fold in. Fry dessertspoons of mixture until golden brown. Serves 4.

Glazed Hawaiian Ham Steaks

4 200g ham steaks
2 tablespoons brown sugar
4 slices tinned pineapple
1 tablespoon butter
2 teaspoons ground ginger

Nick the fat all round the steaks, then coat steaks and pineapple with mixture of brown sugar & ginger. Melt butter in frying pan, add steaks & pineapple slices, cook 3-5 minutes each side or until golden brown.

Hungarian Goulash

2 large onions finely diced
1kg pork shoulder cubed
1 tablespoon ground paprika
Salt & pepper to taste
20g butter
100g plain flour
200ml sour cream

Sautee onions in the butter until transparent. Add paprika, salt & pepper, simmer 5 minutes. Add pork, cover, cook 30 minutes. Sprinkle in flour, stir in, then add sour cream and cook 15 minutes. Serve with boiled potatoes.

Tournedos Rossini

4 tournedos - 100g slices eye fillet steak
4 thick slices liverwurst or pate
4 croutons fried in butter
40g butter

Mushroom Madeira Sauce

200g sliced mushrooms
1 shallot finely chopped
50ml Madeira or dry sherry
200ml beef stock or cubes
Salt & pepper to taste
30g butter
30g plain flour

Heat butter until sizzling, add tournedos and saute each side to preference from rare to well done. Saute pate slices in pan juices. Place each tournedo on a fried bread crouton about 60m round. Place pate on tournedo and glaze with mushroom madeira sauce. Always served 2 to a serve.

Mushroom Madeira Sauce

Cook mushrooms in pan juices and butter until golden, remove from pan. Saute shallots, blend in flour then beef stock, add wine and simmer for 5-6 minutes. Add mushrooms and serve.

Wiener Schnitzel

4 X 150g veal steaks cut thinly	50g plain flour
100g coarse breadcrumbs	Oil for frying
30g butter	1 egg, beaten
Lemon slices & capers	Salt & pepper

Flatten steaks with rolling pin or meat mallet until very thin. Season with salt & pepper both sides, dip first into flour, then egg, finally breadcrumbs. Press with heel of hand to firm coating. Heat enough butter and oil to cover base of heavy frying pan, when sizzling add veal. Cook until brown, turning 3 times during cooking. Serve with slices of lemon and garnish with few capers. Serves 4.

Creme Caramel

Caramel

1/2 cup water	200g sugar

Custard

100ml cream	3 eggs
100ml milk	2 egg yolks
1 piece vanilla pod	50g sugar

Caramel   Put water & sugar in pan over low heat until dissolved. Bring to boil, cook until golden brown. Pour into a large mould or 6 small moulds, and cover bottom.

Custard   Scald cream, milk & vanilla. Cool slightly. Beat whole eggs, yolks & sugar until well blended, pour in milk gradually while stirring. Pour custard into caramel lined mould and set in pan of hot water. Bake in moderate oven for about 45 minutes, or until custard sets. Cool, then chill in refrigerator several hours. Unmould onto serving dish and serve with fresh whipped cream.

Zabaglione

For each person allow:
2 egg yolks, 2 teaspoons sugar, and 15 ml marsala

Beat yolks & sugar until white and fluffy. Stir in marsala. Place mixture over a pan of 'not boiling' water on low heat, whip constantly until frothy and slightly thick. Take care not to boil or it will curdle. As soon as it thickens, pour into warm glasses and serve immediately. Serves 4.

Strawberries Romanoff

2 oranges	170ml curacao
8 sugar lumps	200ml Cream Chantilly
2 punnets strawberries	Vanilla to taste

Cream Chantilly
200ml cream, sugar & vanilla to taste. Whip until firm.

Rub sugar lumps over oranges until they are well impregnated. Crush sugar. Wash and stalk strawberries, soak in curacao & sugar for 2 hours. Put into serving dish with marinade juices. Fold in cream chantilly and serve.

Rice Cream

200g rice	200ml cream
750ml milk	20g castor sugar
Glace cherries	

Heat milk. Simmer rice in milk until tender and all milk is absorbed. Whip cream stiffly with sugar and stir into rice. Pile into bowl and decorate with cherries.

A popular cocktail was # Brandy Crusta

30ml brandy	10ml curacao
Crushed ice	20ml fresh orange juice

Dip the rim of a champagne glass in orange juice, dip in sugar. Lightly shake the ice, brandy, curacao & orange juice, pour and serve garnished with 1/2 slice orange and a glace cherry.

Lemon Meringue Pie

Pastry

80g butter	1 egg	70g sugar
80g SR flour	80g plain flour	5ml vanilla essence

Filling

3 egg yolks	grated rind & juice of 2 lemons
100g sugar	40g plain flour 50ml water

Meringue

3 egg whites	100g sugar	Pinch cream of tartar

Pastry

Cream together butter, sugar & vanilla, add egg, beat well, stir in flour. Turn on to floured surface, knead lightly. Chill 1 hour. Roll out to fit a 150mm pie dish, pinch edges and prick base well with fork. Bake in hot oven until golden brown, allow to cool.

Filling

In top of double saucepan mix egg yolks, sugar, flour, lemon rind, gradually stir in lemon juice & water. Cook, stirring, over boiling water until mixture is smooth and thick. Cool; pour into pie shell.

Meringue

Beat egg whites & cream of tartar until thick, gradually adding sugar until sugar dissolves and mixture is thick. Spread over filling in pie crust, seal completely with meringue. Bake in moderate oven for 8-10 minutes or until meringue is brown.

The mid-seventies saw a growing multi-cultural society in Australia, and many types of Asian food became well known. Specialty restaurants opened, and specialist ingredients became available. During this time Australians discovered quiche and gazpacho soup, and the Western restaurants were being challenged by more discerning palates - and changing from their Australianised cuisine to the purer and classical dishes of their countries of origin. This has given us a large choice of superb dishes from around the world.

Satay

Commonly served in restaurants and at roadside
stalls in Malaysia, Singapore and Indonesia.
Unfamiliar ingredients can be found in Asian spice shops.
1.5kg beef, mutton, pork or chicken, or mix meats
36 bamboo skewers

Cut meat in 40mm X 15mm strips, skewer lengthwise on bamboo skewers, place in a container and pour marinade over. Refrigerate at least 3 hours. To cook, place skewers under grill or on barbeque, turn regularly until cooked, brushing with marinade. Serve on saffron rice; ladle sauce over skewers and serve. Makes 36.

Marinade

1 tablespoon ground coriander
1 teaspoon ground fennel
1-1/2 teaspoons ground cumin
3 cloves garlic, crushed
1 teaspoon turmeric powder
1/2 litre water
1 teaspoon powdered chillies
1 stalk lemon grass chopped
2.5cm chopped fresh ginger
2 teaspoons sugar
1 teaspoon tamarind

Mix coriander, fennel & cumin; dry fry briefly in pan, add garlic, chillies, lemon grass, ginger, sugar, tamarind & turmeric; add water.

Satay Sauce

2 teaspoons ground coriander
1 teaspoon ground cumin
2 teaspoons ground chilli
1-1/2 teaspoons shrimp paste
150g roasted peanuts, crushed
100ml thick coconut milk
75ml tamarind water made with 2 teaspoons tamarind powder
2 cloves garlic, chopped
3 shallots, chopped
8 candle nuts
1 stalk lemongrass
1 tablespoon oil
Sugar & salt to taste

Dry blend coriander, cumin, fennel, chillies, garlic, shallots, dried shrimp paste, candle nuts & lemon grass; heat one tablespoon oil in pan and fry dry seasonings about 3 minutes. Add ground peanuts and stir in coconut milk. Cook on moderate heat, stirring, for 6 minutes. Pour in tamarind water, sugar & salt to taste; add more coconut milk if too thick.

Saffron Rice

1/2 teaspoon saffron strands
25ml boiling water
Salt & pepper to taste

345g long grain rice
50g ghee or oil

Infuse saffron in boiling water and wash rice well. Heat ghee (clarified butter) in heavy bottomed saucepan, put in rice, fry 5 minutes stirring constantly. Cover with 2.5cm water above the level of the rice, strain saffron water and add. Bring to boil, cover, turn to low heat, simmer until all liquid is absorbed and rice is tender. Stand 10 minutes before serving.

Fried Rice (Nasi Goreng)

50g ham or bacon chopped
150g cooked prawns or shrimps
40ml peanut or cooking oil
750g cold cooked white rice
3 spring onions, sliced
1 teaspoon chilli powder

5 sliced spring onions
3 sliced fresh red chillies
10ml soy sauce
2 eggs lightly beaten
100g cooked green peas

Saute spring onions & chillies in 20ml oil. Add chopped bacon or ham and prawns, stir fry 2 minutes. Pour in rice, rest of oil, and sprinkle soy sauce to taste. Stir fry until rice changes colour and is crisp. Keep warm.

Oil pan, pour in beaten egg, cook to a thin omelette, then shred. Add spring onions & peas, heat through. Add rice & chilli powder, stir on high heat for 2 minutes. Spoon onto serving dish and garnish with shredded omelette.

Japanese Marinade Beef Teriyaki

500g porterhouse steak
30ml dark soy sauce
30ml mirin or sweet sherry
3 cloves garlic, crushed

30 ml sake
25g sugar
25g fresh ginger, grated
Wasabi horseradish

Remove all muscle sheathing and fat from beef. Partly freeze until firm then slice as thinly as possible, about 1 mm thick (best to use a meat slicer). Make marinade by combining soy, ginger, garlic, sake, sugar and sherry; cover sliced beef and marinade overnight. Place 3 or 4 slices on a plate and ladle small amount of marinade over. Garnish with wasabi horseradish on side. Serve with chopsticks. Serves 6.

Vietnamese Clay Pot Squid
(Muc Noi Thit)

3 large spring onions
250g finely minced pork
20ml fish sauce
40g tinned sliced bamboo shoots
150ml chicken stock or cubes
4 dried black mushrooms soaked in 100ml water

12 small squid
2 cloves garlic mashed
1 medium carrot, sliced
10ml caramelised sugar

Clean squid, cut off heads. Keep half the tentacles and chop finely, mix with pork, garlic, 2 spring onions, 2 mushrooms, 10ml fish sauce, sugar, salt & pepper. Stuff into squid tube, secure openings with toothpicks. Place in casserole or clay pot with sliced carrot, bamboo shoots and remaining onion cut in 5cm lengths. Quarter remaining mushrooms and liquid, add with caramelised sugar, chicken stock and remaining fish sauce; bake in hot oven 30 minutes. Serve with steamed rice. Serves 4.

Seafood Steamboat
(Lau Do Bien)

4 medium squid tubes
4 young bok choy vegetables
8 dried Chinese mushrooms, soaked
50g tinned sliced bamboo shoots
60g rice noodles soaked & drained
Soy sauce
20ml fish sauce
1-1/2 litres fish or chicken stock, or make with cubes

12 medium prawns
12 scallops
100g fresh bean sprouts
8 slices fresh ginger
3 spring onions
4 eggs, shells washed

Fish Balls

500g white fish   100ml fish sauce   1 egg white

Chop fish fillets and blend with fish sauce, salt, pepper & egg white; process to a smooth paste. Boil pot of water and drop in teaspoonsful of fish paste, simmer until they float; remove. Skin, clean and slice squid tubes, arrange seafood, fish balls, drained mushrooms, vegetables & drained noodles on separate plates for each diner. In a steamboat or improvised tabletop cooker (an old fondu cooker or the like) bring 1-1/2 litres stock to boil, add ginger & spring onions. Each diner cooks own food, retrieving it with chop sticks. Use soy sauce for dipping. Finish meal with eggs and soup.

Indian Tandoori Chicken

1 teaspoon turmeric powder
2 teaspoons chilli powder
1 teaspoon ground fenugreek seeds
3 cloves garlic, chopped
3 teaspoons ground coriander
2 teaspoons black mustard seeds
1/2 teaspoon red food colouring powder
50g dried green mango powder

4 chicken breasts
3 dried chillies
Juice of 1 lemon
2 teaspoons salt
1 teaspoon cumin
1 small onion, grated

To make marinade, place all ingredients other than chicken breasts in a container, and blend.

Skin chicken breasts, slice in 40mm X 15mm strips, skewer on bamboo skewers. Soak in marinade overnight. Remove and cook marinade, reducing to sauce consistency. Grill or barbeque chicken skewers, basting with sauce. Serve with lemon wedges on saffron rice. Serves 4.

Sushi

Rice
Sugar
Carrot
Pickled horseradish root
Dried laver (Nori) seaweed paper
Pickled wasabi horseradish

Vinegar
Salt
Cucumber
Pickled ginger
Spring onion
Soy sauce

Wash rice in cold water, place in heavy based saucepan. Cover with cold water to 4cm above level of rice, bring to boil; turn heat right down, cook until liquid absorbed and rice is tender. Leave stand 10 minutes, then place in large mixing bowl, sprinkle on vinegar, sugar, salt; stir lightly with chopstick. Leave to cool.

Slice finely in 3mm strips: carrot, cucumber (with skin), pickled horseradish root, pickled ginger and spring onion. Place dried laver (Nori) seaweed on flexible bamboo mat, cover with 5m of rice, pressing on with wet hands, leaving a 3cm border of uncovered nori at one end. Arrange strips cucumber, pickled ginger, carrot, pickled horseradish root and spring onion crosswise and roll with mat toward uncovered border. Stick down end of nori with a little soy sauce. Leave for 1 hour to firm, then slice into 15mm rings. Serve with small bowl of dipping soy sauce and wasabi.

Gazpacho Soup

(Cold)

750g ripe tomatoes	1/2 teaspoon ground cumin
1 large white onion	1/2 teaspoon ground black pepper
1 peeled cucumber	80g fine breadcrumbs
100ml Virgin olive oil	1 green pepper (capsicum)
2 cloves garlic	150ml wine vinegar
Salt	100ml iced water

Dice finely tomatoes, onion, cucumber and green pepper. Crush garlic with salt. Add cumin & pepper, mix in breadcrumbs then stir in oil. Add vinegar gradually, then water; add diced vegetables. Refrigerate to marinade for 2 hours before serving.

Quiche Lorraine

Quiche

3-4 rashers bacon	1 teaspoon plain flour
3-4 slices Gruyere cheese	1/2 teaspoon salt
Pinch cayenne pepper	2 eggs
1 tablespoon melted butter	60ml cream
Watercress to garnish	60ml milk

Flan Case

100g plain flour	1 egg yolk
Pinch salt	30ml iced water
Pinch baking powder	Juice 1 lemon
50g butter	

Trim rind off bacon, grill until crisp; cut in 1cm squares. Cut cheese same·size as bacon, place in layers in pastry case. Beat eggs, flour, nutmeg, salt, cayenne, milk and cream; stir in melted butter, pour over bacon & cheese. Bake in hot oven 10 minutes, 200°c, then reduce to 175°c for further 20 minutes. Garnish with watercress and serve warm.

Short Pastry Flan Case

Sift baking powder, flour and salt into bowl. Beat egg yolk, 10ml water, lemon juice, and add to dry mix. Stir into a dough, *knead lightly*, wrap and chill 20 minutes. Roll out and line 200mm pan. Chill again, brush with egg white before putting wet ingredients in.

Cheese Souffle

400ml milk	20 ml cream
1 bay leaf	60g butter
4 egg whites	3 egg yolks
40g grated Parmesan cheese	20g flour
80g grated Parmesan cheese	Pinch nutmeg

Infuse bay leaf in hot milk over low heat 10 minutes. Melt butter in heavy saucepan, remove from heat, add flour, stir well with wooden spoon. Remove bay leaf from milk, cool slightly, then pour over flour mixture; whisk briskly over moderate heat until boiling. Add salt & pepper to taste. Add egg yolks, 80g grated Parmesan cheese, cream & nutmeg while heating.

Whip egg whites until stiff; fold gently and quickly into mixture. Place in souffle dishes lined with foil to create a collar twice as high as the dish; sprinkle 40g cheese & nutmeg, bake in oven 165°c 30 minutes. Serves 4.

Smoked Salmon Mousse

1 tablespoon gelatine	150g smoked salmon
60ml water	100ml whipped cream
2 teaspoons sugar	1 teaspoon salt
1 teaspoon dry mustard	60ml white vinegar

Sprinkle gelatine over water, add sugar, salt, mustard & vinegar. Stir over light heat until gelatine dissolves. Remove from heat and chill until nearly setting; put in salmon and blend until smooth. Fold in whipped cream, then turn into mould(s) and refrigerate. To release from mould, dip mould only in hot water for 3 seconds. Turn out on plate and serve with hot buttered brown toast.

Waldorf Astoria Salad

3 red apples	60 ml mayonnaise
Juice 2 lemons	15 ml cream
150ml sliced celery	6 whole walnuts
100g chopped walnuts	

Quarter apples, remove cores and slice crosswise in 2mm slices; leave peel on for colour. Squeeze lemon juice over to stop browning. Combine all ingredients and serve, garnishing with the whole walnuts.

Risotto of Asparagus,
Scallops & Lemon Balm

36 scallops (roe on)
60ml dry white wine
40ml fresh cream
20ml olive oil
1 onion, finely chopped
2 cloves garlic, chopped

150g short grained rice
800ml fish stock or chicken cubes
16 to 20 asparagus tips only 40mm
Salt & pepper to taste
50g shredded lemon balm

Wash scallops. Pour wine into heavy based pan and simmer; poach scallops 1 minute, remove, reserve liquid. Blanch asparagus tips in boiling salted water 3 minutes, then immerse in ice water until cool; drain and set aside. Heat olive oil in large saucepan, saute onion over low heat until translucent, add garlic and cook lightly. Add rice, stir until well coated; add reserved liquid, stir and cook until absorbed. Add fish stock and cook until rice is aldente; add cream, stir until absorbed. Add scallops and asparagus to hot rice and gently stir in lemon balm. Garnish with scallop shells and lemon balm. Serves 6.

Pears Norzola - Stilton

425g half pears in syrup   200g Norzola Blue or Stilton

Place pears on oven tray split side up; put a slice of norzola (or stilton) on top of each, and grill until pear is warm and cheese is melted. Serve two to a serve. Serves 4.

Fish Fillets Steamed in Paperbark for One

200g fillet of fish (Atlantic salmon, Barramundi, or the like)
12 native pepper leaves   3 small slices lemon peel
Salt & pepper to taste   1 teaspoon olive oil
1 rectangle of paperbark large enough to wrap fillet

Place paperbark on bench, make bed of half pepper leaves. Season, put fish on leaves, strew other leaves and lemon peel; sprinkle olive oil over. Wrap with paperbark and tie with string. Sprinkle water over baking tray to form steam, put fish on and bake in oven 15 minutes, 200°c. Serve unwrapped on plate.

Wattle Mousse

250ml milk   3 eggs, separated
1/4 cup castor sugar   1/4 cup wattle seed mix
1-1/2 tablespoons gelatine   750ml cream

Soak gelatine in enough water to make a paste. Mix wattle seed and half sugar with milk, and bring to boil while stirring. Mix egg yolks with remaining sugar and pour into hot milk; add gelatine paste while stirring. Whip cream slightly (not stiff), whip egg whites until firm. Fold cream and egg whites into cooled wattle seed milk; pour into mould(s), refrigerate few hours. Serve with dollop of cream.

Wattle Tea

1 heaped teaspoon of wattle seeds per cup

Dry roast seeds in a saucepan over heat several minutes but don't burn. Add water, bring to boil, strain and serve with or without milk and sugar to taste, or serve cold.

Native Currant Dressing

200g native currants   140ml macadamia oil
1 egg yolk

Combine ingredients in a food processor, refrigerate. Can be used warm or cold.

Lillipilli Vinegar

2kg lillipilli fruit   3 litres white wine vinegar

Simmer fruit and vinegar 2 hours. Allow to cool, then strain and bottle. Has delightful oriental spice flavour.

Rosella Relish

(Rosella is not the parrot, but the calyx of hibiscus)

1kg wild rosella, seeds removed   200g sultanas
3 large Spanish onions, sliced   300ml malt vinegar
200g small leaved lillipilli fruit   100g sugar
salt, pepper & native pepper to taste   Cooking oil

Fry onions in little oil, add rosella and lillipilli, cover with water. Boil 15 minutes, add sugar, vinegar & sultanas; simmer 1 hour. Add seasonings to taste, and bottle.

Warrigal Greens and Potato Soup

200g warrigal greens   1 litre vegetable stock or water
1 brown onion, chopped   1 clove garlic
200g potatoes, peeled   Salt and pepper to taste

Blanch and chop greens. Sautee onion; add stock and potatoes; boil until potato breaks down. Add greens, garlic, and season. Simmer 30 minutes and serve.

Witchetty Grub Soup

20 fresh grubs   100g leeks, sliced
1 clove garlic   2 litres chicken stock
80ml cooking oil   Salt & pepper to taste
Little flour   100ml cream

Sautee leek & garlic, then add grubs and sautee slowly. Add stock, cook 1 hour. Blend then bring back to boil; add paste made by mixing oil and flour, gradually stirring until thick (use only as much as you need), add cream and serve.

An industrial canteen kitchen during the 1920's. A roast & veg. being served.

Grilled Loin of Lamb

(With greens and red currant sauce)

2 loins about 500g, boned, trimmed of all fat
Salt & pepper to taste   30ml peanut oil
150g red currants, fresh or frozen   4 cloves garlic
30ml balsamic vinegar   4 sprigs thyme
200g greens
(dandelion, mizuna, purslane, curly endive or spinach)

Preheat oven 250°c. Cut lamb into 4 pieces, heat heavy skillet to smoking, add 15ml oil and sear lamb on all sides. Keeping lamb in skillet, drain and discard oil, add 2 cloves garlic and the thyme; put in oven 8 minutes. Meanwhile chop finely remaining garlic. Take skillet from oven, remove lamb and keep warm. Add 1/2 cup water to skillet, boil to reduce by half, add crushed currants, reduce to a glaze, strain and keep warm. Reheat skillet, add remaining oil, minced garlic and greens, tossing rapidly. Add vinegar and toss until greens are barely wilted. Divide between 4 plates; slice lamb and arrange beside greens. Spoon red currant sauce over lamb and serve. Serves 4.

Atlantic Salmon & Chervil

4 100g salmon fillets   1kg new potatoes (pinkeyes)
1/2 bunch chervil   80ml white wine vinegar
1 shallott, chopped   80g butter
80ml cream

Cook salmon on barbeque, under griller, or best on webber cooker. Meanwhile heat little butter in small pan, saute shallott, add vinegar and boil until reduced to one third. Add cream and reduce until slightly thickened; whip in rest of butter, strain and keep warm. Cook potatoes in salted water until 3/4 done; strain, slice and place as bed on serving plates. Place cooked salmon on potatoes. Chop chervil finely, add to sauce, then pour over fish and serve. Serves 4.

Smoked Salmon & Caviar Pizza

Pizza Dough

1 small pack yeast   1 teaspoon honey
100ml warm water   100g plain flour
1 teaspoon salt   30ml olive oil

Put water in small bowl, dissolve yeast and honey. Combine flour, yeast and honey water, and oil, kneading well and adding water until dough is firm. Allow to rise in covered bowl in warm place for 30 minutes. Then divide into 170g balls; work each ball by pulling down on sides & tucking underneath about 5 times. On unfloured surface roll ball under hand until smooth and firm. Cover with damp towel and allow to rise 15 minutes. They can be refrigerated or used immediately.

Pizza Topping

150g smoked salmon   200g brie or Camembert cheese
80g sour cream   1 tablespoon golden caviar
30ml olive oil
4 kitchen or bathroom tiles about 17cm to 20cm square

Heat tiles in oven 15 minutes, 250°c. Roll pizza dough into four 17cm circles, brush with oil, slice cheese thinly and cover pizzas. Slide onto hot tiles, bake in oven 8 - 12 minutes or until crust golden brown. Take tiles from oven, remove pizzas and place on serving plates. Spread pizzas with sour cream, cover with finely sliced smoked salmon; put clot of sour cream in centre and divide the caviar, add sour cream and serve. Serves 4.

The 1990's are an exciting time in the evolving Australian Cuisine. One development is in bush tucker - Australian native fruits, seeds and flavourings which are becoming commercially available and which are appearing in gourmet food shops. Innovative chefs are developing flavours uniquely Australian.

Californian cuisine combines Asian and European influences with the accent on fresh. For summer, and for warmer climates, Italian dishes with pestos, sundried tomatoes, virgin olive oils, balsamic or flavoured vinegars, are a world-wide trend.

The 1990's are the health conscious decade, and Australians are eating lighter and healthier. The range of fresh vegetables has increased; for example, over 8 varieties of lettuce are commonly stocked. Meat is being trimmed of fat and grown leaner yet tender. The trend is to undercooking vegetables, and not overcooking fish, poultry and meat - helped by Japanese sushimis taking the fear out of eating raw meat and fish.

Grilled Shitake Mushroom Salad

12 large shitake mushrooms
1 cup extra virgin olive oil
1 tablespoon Worcestershire sauce
1/2 tablespoon Dijon mustard
1 cup balsamic vinegar
250g assorted lettuce
Greens (mescal mix)
Salt & pepper to taste

Make marinade of Worcestershire sauce, 2 tablespoons vinegar, 3 tablespoons oil, salt & pepper; toss de-stemmed mushroom caps in marinade and stand 2 hours.

Make salad dressing with rest of oil, vinegar and mustard; season to taste.

Grill mushrooms lightly; mix greens and dressing. Slice finely the grilled warm mushrooms and sprinkle over salad.

Olive Oil Mayonnaise

1 cup vinegar
1 tablespoon tarragon
1 cup white wine
1 bay leaf
1 clove garlic
1/4 cup cornflour & water paste
1 teaspoon English mustard powder
Juice 2 lemons
6 egg yolks
350ml olive oil (the better the quality, the better the result)

Put vinegar, tarragon, wine & bay leaf in small pot over heat; reduce by half. Strain, return to heat, thicken with cornflour, then chill. Place mixture in mixer or blender with egg yolks, mustard, garlic & lemon juice. Blend, gradually adding oil in thin stream until mayonnaise is thick. Cover and refrigerate.

Vegetarian Salad with Grilled Eggplant & Green Zucchini

6 X 60g eggplants	6 X 60g green zucchinis
30ml olive oil	30ml mint sauce
60g mixed lettuce leaves	180g tomato salsa
1 onion, chopped	20 basil leaves
1 clove garlic	4 basil leaves
Juice 2 lemons	

180g marinated button mushrooms
1 teaspoon pink peppercorns, ground black pepper and mustard

Blend garlic, peppercorns, pepper, mustard, 20 basil leaves, lemon juice and mint sauce. Cut thin slices of zucchini and eggplant; dribble with olive oil and lightly grill. Make tomato salsa by blending tomatoes, onion and 4 basil leaves.

Spoon tomato salsa onto plate, swill around until base of plate is covered. Arrange lettuce leaves on one side and grilled zucchini and eggplant on the other side, with the dressing in a small jug. Serves 6.

Aioli

(To be used as a dip or spread on bread as a side dish with a meal)

2 cups olive oil mayonnaise   6 cloves garlic, peeled

Combine mayonnaise & garlic; blend until smooth.

Pesto

(To be used as a dip or placed on thin slices of bread stick and toasted)

50g pine nuts	salt & pepper to taste
10 young basil leaves	3 cloves garlic
1/2 cup grated parmesan	100ml olive oil

Put all ingredients in blender, then process until coarse, then while processing gradually add olive oil until smooth but with some texture.

Game Consomme with Poached Quail Egg

Carcase of 1 quail and 1 pheasant, with 4 boned venison ribs
Meat of the above roughly chopped

1 quail egg per serve	1 carrot
4 cloves garlic	1 onion
2 tomatoes, chopped	4 egg whites
1/2 litre white wine	Salt & pepper to taste

Roast bones and meat in hot oven 250°c until browned. In large stock pot heat little olive oil, adding chopped tomatoes, onion, carrot and garlic; cook until coloured. Add bones & meat, cover with water; add wine. Bring to boil then simmer 4-1/2 hours, skimming fat & scum regularly. Strain & clarify by whipping the egg whites through the broth, then strain again. Adjust seasoning; bring to boil; put in soup bowls. Crack a quail egg into each bowl of hot consomme and allow to set then serve.

Lemon Iced Souffle with Raspberry Coulis

1 cup castor sugar	5 egg whites
1 cup water	2/3 cup lemon butter
1 cup lightly whipped cream	

Lemon Butter:

250g butter	250g sugar
Juice 5 lemons	3 eggs

Raspberry Coulis:

250g pureed raspberries	1/4 cup sugar

Souffle:

Heat castor sugar in water until dissolved. Beat egg whites until peaking; pour dissolved sugar into egg whites while beating or blending; keep beating until cooled, then chill. Soften butter, cream & 250g sugar; add lemon juice and eggs. Cook over double boiler, stirring constantly until thick. Fold two mixtures together, place in souffle dishes and chill.

Take the souffles out of dishes and pool raspberry coulis around them on individual plates.

Onion Comfits with Barramundi or Trevalla Fillet

200g fish fillets (2)
150g pearl onions
10ml vinegar
200ml fish stock
100g butter
10g lemon zest
1 teaspoon crushed black peppercorns
12g carrots
15g honey
2 cloves garlic, chopped
45ml Sauterne
6 chives

Brush fish with butter and layer with julienne of carrot; season and steam lightly. Sautee onions in butter until soft, then bake with honey and vinegar 20 minutes, 180°c. Sweat chopped shallots in butter; add pepper, fish stock, sauterne; over heat reduce by half. Mix in butter, add onions, honey & vinegar. Place around fish on plate and serve. Serves 2.

Mancha Manteles
(Pork with Bananas & Peaches)

500g pork
3 bananas, peeled, sliced
3 peaches, peeled, sliced
2 cloves
1/2 teaspoon ground black pepper
Chillies, salt, pepper & sugar to taste
4 cloves garlic
1/2 onion chopped finely
1 cinnamon stick
1/2 cup water

Make sauce first: place cloves. onion, garlic, pepper & chilli in saucepan with 1/2 cup water. Cook until soft then puree until smooth; add more water if needed.

Heat some olive oil in heavy skillet; saute pork; remove, then sautee bananas. Replace pork in skillet with bananas; add sauce and peaches. Simmer 10 minutes, adjusting seasoning with pepper, salt and sugar. Serves 4.

Veal in Balsamic Vinegar

600g medallions of veal
1 cup beef stock
4 tablespoons balsamic vinegar
flour, salt, mace, butter, pepper

Dust veal in flour; cook in hot buttered skillet both sides, then add stock, balsamic vinegar, pepper, salt, pinch nutmeg; serve. Serves 4.

Some Quick Cup Measures

1 cup of:

flour	150g	fresh breadcrumbs	60g
white sugar	210g	dry breadcrumbs	125g
icing sugar	150g	biscuit crumbs	105g
brown sugar	150g	rice, raw	180g
butter	210g	mixed fruit	185g
honey	360g	nuts, chopped	125g
coconut, dried	90g	cheddar cheese, grated	150g

Measures

LIQUID		SOLID	
Imperial	Metric	Ounces	Grams
1 teaspoon	5ml	1oz	30g
1 tablespoon	20ml	4oz (1/4lb)	125g
2 fluid oz (1/4 cup)	62.5ml	8oz (1/2lb)	250g
4 fluid oz (1/2 cup)	125ml	12oz (3/4lb)	375g
8 fluid oz (1 cup)	250ml	16oz (1lb)	500g
1 pint (20 fluid oz/2½ cups)	625ml	24oz (1½lb)	750g
1 pint (US & Canada) (16 fluid oz)	500ml	32oz (2lb)	1kg

Cake Tins

6 inch - 15 cm   Loaf Tin: 9" x 5" - 23 x 12 cm
7 inch - 18 cm   Bar Tin: 10" x 3" - 25 x 8 cm
9 inch - 23 cm   Lamington: 11" x 7" - 28 x 18 cm

Oven Temperature Guide

	Electric		Gas		
	°C	°F	°C	°F	Mark
Cool	110	225	100	200	1/4
Very Slow	120	250	120	250	1/2
Slow	150	300	150	300	1 - 2
Moderately Slow	170	340	160	325	3
Moderate	200	400	180	350	4
Moderately Hot	220	425	190	375	5 - 6
Hot	230	450	200	400	6 - 7
Very Hot	250	475	230	450	8 - 9

CUP AND SPOON EQUIVALENTS IN OUNCES & GRAMS

INGREDIENT	1/2oz 15g	1oz 30g	2oz 60g	3oz 90g	4oz 125g	5oz 150g	6oz 180g	7oz 210g	8oz 250g
Almonds:									
ground	2T	1/4C	1/2C	3/4C	1-1/4C	1-1/3C	1-2/3C	2C	2-1/4C
Apples, dried	3T	1/2C	1C	1-1/3C	2C	2-1/3C	2-3/4C	3-1/3C	3-3/4C
Apricots:									
chopped	2T	1/4C	1/2C	3/4C	1C	1-1/4C	1-1/2C	1-3/4C	2C
whole	2T	3T	1/2C	2/3C	1C	1-1/4C	1-1/3C	1-1/2C	1-3/4C
Arrowroot	1T	2T	1/3C	1/2C	2/3C	3/4C	1C	1-1/4C	1-1/3C
Baking Pdr	1T	2T	1/3C	1/2C	2/3C	3/4C	1C	1C	1-1/4C
Barley	1T	2T	1/4C	1/2C	2/3C	3/4C	1C	1C	1-1/4C
Bicarb. Soda	1T	2T	1/3C	1/2C	2/3C	3/4C	1C	1C	1-1/4C
Breadcrumbs:									
dry	2T	1/4C	1/2C	3/4C	1C	1-1/4C	1-1/2C	1-3/4C	2C
soft	1/4C	1/2C	1C	1-1/2C	2C	2-1/2C	3C	3-2/3C	4-1/4C
Biscuit Crumbs	2T	1/4C	1/2C	3/4C	1-1/4C	1-1/3C	1-2/3C	2C	2-1/4C
Butter	3t	6t	1/4C	1/3C	1/2C	2/3C	3/4C	1C	1C
Cheese grated:									
nat. cheddar	6t	1/4C	1/2C	3/4C	1C	1-1/4C	1-1/2C	1-3/4C	2C
proc. cheddar	5t	2T	1/3C	2/3C	3/4C	1C	1-1/4C	1-1/2C	1-2/3C
Parmesan and									
Romano	6t	1/4C	1/2C	3/4C	1C	1-1/3C	1-2/3C	2C	2-1/4C
Cherries glace									
chopped	1T	2T	1/3C	1/2C	3/4C	1C	1C	1-1/3C	1-1/2C
whole	1T	2T	1/3C	1/2C	2/3C	3/4C	1C	1-1/4C	1-3/4C
Cocoa	2T	1/4C	1/2C	3/4C	1-1/4C	1-1/3C	1-2/3C	2C	2-1/4C
Coconut, dried	2T	1/3C	2/3C	1C	1-1/3C	1-2/3C	2C	2-1/3C	2-2/3C
shredded	1/3C	2/3C	1-1/4C	1-3/4C	2-1/2C	3C	3-2/3C	4-1/3C	5C
Cornflour	6t	3T	1/2C	2/3C	1C	1-1/4C	1-1/2C	1-2/3C	2C
Coffee: ground	2T	1/3C	2/3C	1C	1-1/3C	1-2/3C	2C	2-1/3C	2-2/3C
instant	3T	1/2C	1C	1-1/3C	1-3/4C	2-1/4C	2-2/3C	3C	3-1/2C
Cornflakes	1/2C	1C	2C	3C	4-1/4C	5-1/4C	6-1/4C	7-1/3C	8-1/3C
Cream of Tartar	1T	2T	1/3C	1/2C	2/3C	3/4C	1C	1C	1-1/4C
Currants	1T	2T	1/3C	2/3C	3/4C	1C	1-1/4C	1-1/2C	1-2/3C
Custard Powdr.	6t	3T	1/2C	2/3C	1C	1-1/4C	1-1/2C	1-2/3C	2C
Dates, choppd	1T	2T	1/3C	2/3C	3/4C	1C	1-1/4C	1-1/2C	1-2/3C
whole, pitted	1T	2T	1/3C	1/2C	3/4C	1C	1-1/4C	1-1/3C	1-1/2C
Figs, chopped	1T	2T	1/3C	1/2C	3/4C	1C	1C	1-1/3C	1-1/2C
Flour, SR, plain	6t	1/4C	1/2C	3/4C	1C	1-1/4C	1-1/2C	1-3/4C	2C
wholemeal	6t	3T	1/2C	2/3C	1C	1-1/4C	1-1/3C	1-2/3C	1-3/4C
Fruit, mixed	1T	2T	1/3C	1/2C	3/4C	1C	1-1/2C	1-1/3C	1-1/2C
Gelatine	5t	2T	1/3C	1/2C	3/4C	1C	1C	1-1/4C	1-1/2C
Ginger:									
crystalised	1T	2T	1/3C	1/2C	3/4C	1C	1-1/4C	1-1/3C	1-1/2C
ground	6t	1/3C	1/2C	3/4C	1-1/4C	1-1/2C	1-3/4C	2C	2-1/4C
in syrup	1T	2T	1/3C	1/2C	2/3C	3/4C	1C	1C	1-1/4C
Glucose, liquid	2t	1T	2T	1/4C	1/3C	1/2C	1/2C	2/3C	2/3C
Golden Syrup	2t	1T	2T	1/4C	1/3C	1/2C	1/2C	2/3C	2/3C
Haricot Beans	1T	2T	1/3C	1/2C	2/3C	3/4C	1C	1C	1-1/4C

t = teaspoonful   T = tablespoonful C = cupful